Boundary Waters 101
A Primer for America's Favorite Wilderness

By Jim Rahtz

ISBN-13: 978-1983751806
ISBN-10: 1983751804

Contents

Chapter 1: The Boundary Waters

Henry David Thoreau once said, "Everyone must believe in something. I believe I'll go canoeing." If I could humbly add to Thoreau's quote, I'd state that I believe the best place to go canoeing is within The Boundary Waters.

The Boundary Waters is the common name for two large, separate yet adjacent tracts of land and water. The Boundary Waters Canoe Area Wilderness (BWCAW) contains over one million acres of designated wilderness within Superior National Forest in northeast Minnesota. Just across the border in Ontario, Canada, an additional 1.1 million acres of wilderness exists as Quetico Provincial Park. Together, they form one of the best spots on the planet to canoe, camp, fish, watch wildlife, view pre-historic pictographs, immerse yourself in nature and recharge.

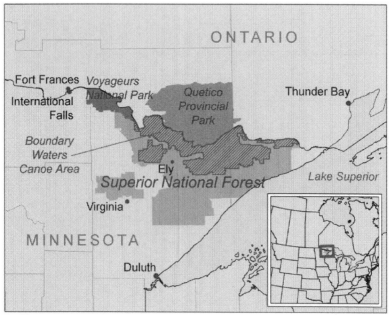

By Kmusser [CC BY-SA 3.0 (https://creativecommons.org/licenses/by-sa/3.0)]

It is hard to grasp the sheer size of the Boundary Waters. There is enough acreage there to cover Central Park in New York 2,500 times. It is four times the size of Great Smoky Mountain National Park. And there is not a single road within it. Boats with motors are restricted to just a few lakes along the periphery. For the most part, all travel through this amazing area is by paddle or foot.

The area has an interesting history. Pictographs and Petrographs throughout the Boundary Waters provide vivid reminders of the prehistoric and historic Ojibwe people that once lived on the land and water.

Frances Ann Hopkins

The first European to visit is thought to be the French explorer Jacques de Noyon in 1688. During the 18th Century, the Famous Voyageurs paddled and portaged through the Boundary Waters hauling trade goods west and furs back east. This portion of the boundary between the U.S. and Canada wasn't actually settled until the mid-1800s; and then based upon the trade route.

Logging and mining began in earnest in the late 1800s, but even then there were those on both sides of the border that saw the greatest value of the area as protected wilderness. In 1909, Superior National Forest was created in Minnesota. On the

Canadian side, Quetico Provincial Park was named that same year.

Through the following decades, protections were added to specific American acreage known as the Superior Roadless Primitive Area. With the passage of the 1964 Wilderness Act, that land, by then named the Boundary Waters Canoe Area, became a unit of the National Wilderness Preservation System.

Despite the designation, major portions of the BWCA were still open for logging, motorboat and snowmobile use. Over the next several years there were judicial actions and legislative attempts to codify the area's protection once and for all. In 1977, Congress held hearings in Minnesota on the future of the BWCA. Sigurd Olson, noted area conservationist, addressed one hearing:

This is the most beautiful lake country on the continent. We can afford to cherish and protect it. Some places should be preserved from development or exploitation for they satisfy a human need for solace, belonging and perspective. In the end we turn to nature in a frenzied chaotic world, there to find silence—oneness—wholeness—spiritual release.

The following year, the 1978 BWCA Wilderness Act was passed. The act guaranteed the continued protection of the land on the American side and set many of the regulations still in use today such as limited motor use on the lakes. From this point on the official name of the area became the Boundary Waters Canoe Area Wilderness (BWCAW).

Many things make the Boundary Waters special and worthy of the special protections afforded to it. At the top of the list is water. Approximately 20% of the entire area is lake or stream. The Boreal forest is thick with pine, fir, spruce and cedar, significant portions of which have never been logged. Deciduous maple, aspen and birch add to the diversity of these north woods. In such a large, contiguous wilderness, wildlife has an opportunity to thrive. Sightings of beaver, otter and eagle are common. Moose and bear occasionally make an appearance and a few lucky visitors may get a glimpse of a wolf. Wolf howls in the distance and the haunting call of the loon add the soundtrack to a trip there.

The lakes are (almost) clean enough to drink from and they harbor world class wilderness fishing for four species. There is cultural history to explore from prehistoric petrographs to remnants of the logging/mining. At night, the absence of light pollution provides a star show second to none, with the added chance of a glimpse of the northern lights. Put it all together and there are tremendous opportunities to reconnect with nature and recharge your soul. Whether you just want to be out in unspoiled wilderness with a group of friends, or take the solitary challenge of being safe and comfortable alone in the wild, the Boundary Waters are waiting for you.

Make no mistake, there are very real challenges you will deal with in the Boundary Waters. No, they are not insurmountable. (For example, yes there are mosquitos. No, they are not the state bird.) This basic introduction is designed to provide you with the information you need to start the decision-making process whether to accept the challenge and plan a trip to this incredible area.

Chapter 2: Decisions

Travel to the BWCAW or Quetico Provincial Park is not like a trip to a state park or an amusement park. By going into the wilderness, you are assuming complete responsibility for your transportation, comfort, food preparation, entertainment and safety. There are no handy stores to pick up odds and ends partway through the journey. Proper planning is key to a successful trip. Much of that planning involves decision-making. "OK" you say, "but what decisions do I need to make?" Glad you asked.

When?

The best time to visit the Boundary Waters is anytime you can. Assuming you are not tied into any specific time for your trip however, there are several items to consider when picking trip dates. The start of the season coincides with ice-out. Although it varies from year to year, the water typically becomes "soft" enough to float a canoe around the first of May. However, this can vary. For example, 2013 and 2014 were both late with ice-out occurring 10 days behind the long-term average. Some lakes were not open until after May 15. At the other end of the season, smaller lakes can start freezing up again in late October. Since getting caught in the wilderness when the lakes can neither be paddled across or walked on can result in a very unenjoyable trip, I'd suggest staying away from trying to catch either the very first or last days of open water.

In between the two extremes, there are a wide variety of times to consider, depending upon the interests and expectations of the group. Different interests can point to different times, so priorities need to be decided. For example, to avoid crowds, stay away from July and early August. However, wanting to have water warm enough to swim points to that very period.

A few things to keep in mind: As far as bugs; mosquitos and black flies are at their worst early in the season, tending to die back by mid-summer. Horse flies and deer flies can last well into August.

No mosquitos on this trip

Wildlife sightings tend to be better when visitation is lower, such as early in the season and in the fall.

The best fishing varies by species. Of the four that most people pursue, lake trout are easiest to find shortly after ice-out before they head deep to avoid the warm water of the summer. Autumn, after Labor Day, provides another shot.

Northern pike and walleye follow the same pattern, but tend to be more forgiving of the timing. The best action can last through June and pick up again in August.

Smallmouth bass are a species that was introduced to the area and stay active in warmer water. They are slow to bite in the early spring, but can provide plenty of action all summer long.

Beyond seasons, consider moon phases as well. The night sky can be quite an attraction all by itself. A full moon is impressive, but when there is no moon, there are more stars on display than you can see anywhere near a city. The Milky Way is on full display. I've even seen satellites streak across the sky. The Northern Lights aren't on a predictable pattern, but are most dazzling when they don't have to compete with the moon.

U.S. or Canada?
This is a big one. Even though the Boundary Waters Canoe Area Wilderness and Quetico Provincial Park are adjacent to each other, there are significant differences to consider when determining which area to visit.

Though neither area is "crowded" by any stretch of the imagination, the BWCAW receives the large majority of the visitation. The approximately 300,000 that visit make it the most visited wilderness area in the U.S. By contrast, only about 10% of that number visit Quetico annually. There's no doubt the Canadian side provides more seclusion, especially on a summer trip. Less visitation also means less fishing pressure, and many believe better odds on hooking into that monster you've been dreaming about.

Why do most visitors stay on the U.S. side? There are a number of reasons for that. First of all, it's handier. The easiest way for Americans to get to Quetico is to go through the BWCAW. If you don't have a strong preference, it makes sense to go to the closest location. It's also simpler. In this post 9/11 world, crossing the border involves getting a passport in addition to dealing with Remote Area Border Crossing Permits and stops at Customs.

There are less permits available for Quetico as well, insuring it is less crowded. Permit and camping fees are more expensive for a trip to Canada, even with what has recently been a strong dollar. For example, let's compare the costs for a five night family trip with two adults and two youth for 2018.

BWCAW:
Permit reservation fee - $10
Camping - $16/adult and $8/youth for a total of $48
Fishing License – Non-resident Family License - $60
Total Fees - $118

Quetico
Permit reservation fee - $15
Remote Area Border Crossing Pass (required for most trips) - $30 per family
Camping - $21.47/adult/**night** and $8.48/youth/**night** for a total of $299.50
Fishing License – Non-resident 8 day (age 17 and over is $30.53) for a total of $61.06
Total Fees – If all one family $405.56
What's the extra seclusion and possibility of better fishing worth? In this instance, almost $300. The Quetico costs are in Canadian Dollars which, as of this writing, are exchanged at about a 20% discount to American Dollars. That brings the costs a bit closer, but still not close.

By the way, there are additional fishing restrictions in Quetico compared with the Boundary Waters as well. No live bait is permitted north of the border and barbless hooks must be used.

Depending upon the makeup of your group, there is one other consideration. In Quetico, you can camp anywhere, though campsites with fire rings are well established where you'd generally want to camp. In the Boundary Waters, only designated campsites are to be used. However, these include fire rings with a cooking grate and a toilet somewhere nearby. Notice I didn't say restroom, latrine or outhouse. There's a toilet set over a hole in the ground. No roof; no walls. However, compared to squatting over a hole you just dug (the Quetico option), the facilities can seem downright plush.

So, costs, crowds, regulations and even the wilderness experience of your morning constitutional should all be considered in choosing your destination.

Route

Another decision? Yes, and this one is important for a whole variety of reasons. What is the perfect trip in your mind? Are you looking to travel a short distance, set up a base camp and spend your time fishing? Or, are you wanting to see as much as possible, traveling every day and covering big miles? Do you want to visit some petrographs and other signs of the area's history?

How much seclusion are you looking for? Even considering the earlier discussion of visitation of the BWCAW versus Quetico, seclusion is possible even in mid-summer in either location. However, to do that, you must get off the beaten path. The more portages you cross, the less people you'll see. Long portages are even better. Multiple long portages into "dead end" lakes (one way in and out) can pretty much guarantee seclusion. You get the picture.

"Portages," you say to yourself. "What is he talking about?" Portage can be a noun or a verb. The land route between lakes or around rapids is called a portage. When you are hauling your canoe and all your "stuff" over that route to the next lake, you are portaging. There are some short, relatively easy portages; and there are portages from hell. In general though, I agree with famous canoeist Bill Mason who said, "Anyone who says they like portaging is either a liar or crazy."

Portages are measured in rods. Each rod is 16 ½ feet

Is everyone in the group of the same mindset, or are there competing priorities? This may be the most important point to consider. If one person wants to spend the days casting for smallies, and another person's dream is to travel and see as much scenery as possible, and they are both on the same trip; one or both may have a lousy time. If at all possible, make sure your group is all on the same page, or at least understands the "plan" for the trip.

Food

There are various schools of thought on this one. Stu Oshoff, publisher of the Boundary Waters Journal, only takes "real" food on the trips he guides. He brings an insulated cooler within a pack and includes perishables like raw meat, salad, milk, cheese and so on to enjoy throughout the trip. That actually sounds really good. It also sounds really heavy. Since I don't have Stu to carry my food across the portages, I look at other options.

As a backpacker, I'm aware of the huge variety of freeze dried meals available. They are lightweight, easy to prepare and will keep for years. What they typically aren't is tasty and satisfying. (I must say, there are a few that I like pretty well though. Test for yourself.) Folks using this method tend to think of food as nothing more than the fuel needed to power themselves through the adventure.

In the end, I'm inclined to follow a middle ground. As I head out, the pack might include frozen steaks, eggs and other perishables, but only enough for the first day or two. The heavy stuff leaves the pack first and I soon switch to crackers and freeze-dried meals. It's either the best or worst of both worlds, depending on how you want to look at it.

The Group

The members of the group will make or break a trip. Consider each member's physical ability when deciding on the miles and portages to be covered. Do members of the group have the skills to be safe and comfortable in the wild or are they counting on you? How does your group handle adversity? You need to remember, portages are not all easy, the sun isn't always shining, there are often bugs to deal with and the fish do not always cooperate. When choosing your group, skills can be important, but a positive attitude and a willingness to work when things aren't going according to plan is priceless.

Outfitter?

Should you use an outfitter? For first timers, I absolutely recommend you let one outfit you. They have all the equipment, experience and knowledge you are going to need. If you already have a canoe or some other equipment you'd like to use, partial outfitting is easily done. I speak from experience here. Looking back, I outfitted myself on my first trip and it was the last trip my first wife and I ever took together. Of course, if you are looking for a reason to argue and possibly split up....

After many trips and purchasing all the equipment needed, I still work with an outfitter. Why? The route. The outfitters I have worked with can put together one that fits various needs and wants of the group, fitting it within the available timeframe. Even if you know generally what route you want to take, a good outfitter can provide essential local knowledge. Outfitters I've dealt with will take maps of your route and mark them up with helpful, and sometimes critical, information you'll need to navigate through the wilderness. Generally, this is a free service if you get complete outfitting and well worth the cost if you're partially or self-outfitting. The best campsites, fishing spots, pictograph locations, waterfalls, optional side trips and even items such as a relocated portage or an island with a history of bear issues have all been marked on maps for me.

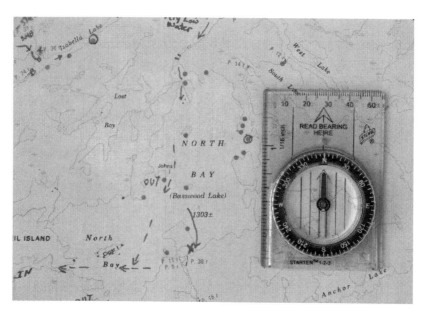

In addition, using an outfitter can have additional benefits. You don't have to worry about where to leave the car. Permits can be handled for you. If you plan to arrive the night before, you can arrange for a room, a hearty breakfast and get an early start. If you're leaving from an area that allows motors, a tow can get you a head start into the wilderness.

Motor tows and even fly-in trips can be arranged

Campsite

An outfitter typically has a deep knowledge of the area and can provide advice about the best campsites. But here, the best site is in the eye of the beholder. If you plan to travel or fish from dawn to dusk each day, a convenient location might be the highest priority for a camp spot. If you plan on spending time at camp relaxing, napping or whatever; the right site can enhance the experience that much more. In no particular order, here are some of the details I look for in the perfect campsite.

- Enough flat area for the group's tents and a tarp free from dead or leaning trees (widow makers).
- An area that is open and receives a breeze to reduce any issue with biting insects. Sites on points of land or islands typically work well. They often have the bonus of good views. If visiting in spring or fall, a more protected site may be in order.

- Many sites have some large rocks that can serve as a kitchen table and keep food preparation off the ground.
- A gentle slope into the water makes for easier loading and unloading of the canoes. If traveling with kids, the right landing can work well as a beach.
- Hoping to see the Northern Lights? Make sure there's an open view towards the north.
- If the reason for the trip is angling, that can be a campsite consideration too. Is there a good spot to cast in the evening? On windy days, a spot to shore fish or a nearby protected bay can suddenly become a real bonus.

Where's the chow? Courtesy Williams and Hall Outfitters

- A nearby tree that lends itself to "bear bagging" your food. It's a good idea to, using rope, tie your food from a branch so the food pack is ten feet in the air and six feet from the trunk of the tree. While bear problems are rare, having one eat your food makes for a bad trip and can result in the bear losing its natural tendency to avoid humans. Keeping the food elevated also reduces the much more likely problem of mice or chipmunks raiding your chow.

Chapter 3: Fishing

Beyond just enjoying being in a wilderness area, the number one reason people visit the Boundary Waters is for the fishing. I've had the best day of fishing in my life on Basswood Lake. Like anywhere else however, there have been days when I couldn't buy a bite.

A number of books have been written about the world class fishing in this area and I won't pretend to be able to add to that store of knowledge myself. However, I can share some of the expertise of Blayne Hall, owner of Williams and Hall Outfitters. They're situated at the edge of the Boundary Waters on Moose Lake. Blayne took his first trip to the Boundary Waters over 30 years ago and has operated Williams and Hall for the last 25.

Blayne Hall, Courtesy Williams and Hall Outfitters

Like many people, Blayne finds fishing in the Boundary Waters to be a special experience. Unlike spending the day in a motorboat and returning to a room or cabin, a multi-day trip into the Boundary Waters provides him a real connection with the outdoors and nature. He also enjoys the higher responsibility of being in the wilderness. Once you enter it, "you're on your own." All this is on top of the fact that the area is a world class fishery.

In his experience, the BWCAW can provide just as high quality of a fishing experience as Quetico. In either location, getting away from entry points and off the more popular travel routes is key; well worth the effort in improved catch rates.

Courtesy Williams and Hall Outfitters

Blayne's general fishing advice is pretty straightforward. First of all: "You can't catch any fish if you're not fishing."

Many visitors travel all day and, by the time camp is set up in the evening, they are too tired to seriously fish. Blayne encourages that fishing become a priority on the trip. There are a few ways to plan more time for fishing. One way is to travel only on the first and last day of the trip. In between, set up a "base camp" and take daily fishing excursions from there. If the plan does involve traveling each day, get up early, travel and set up the next camp by mid-afternoon. That leaves time for some significant fishing each evening. In addition, put at least one layover day into the plan. A layover day allows flexibility if the weather turns ugly and if not; there's one full day available to fish.

Secondly, Blayne advises anglers to "think like a minnow." All four of the major targeted species (lake trout, northern pike, walleye, smallmouth bass) prey on minnows. If you can figure out where the minnows are, the fish you are targeting are probably nearby.

Towards that end, follow the wind and current. Minnows aren't going to fight these forces so that immediately narrows the area to target. Food and cover are priorities for minnows and they can find both on steep rocky shorelines. In the evening these small fish will move into more shallow water, hanging near weeds, grass, rocks and stumps. Larger game fish looking for a tasty dinner will be hunting in the same area.

A point Blayne emphasized to me was the need to be sure of the quality of your equipment. There's a good chance of latching on to real trophy. This is not the place to have an old rod snap or a cheap reel lock up. And put new line on that reel! It's inexpensive insurance.

Over time, each angler develops an affinity for a particular type of outfit. Generically speaking though, a good starter outfit includes a 5 ½ - 6 foot medium to medium light action rod; either in one or two pieces. Match the rod with a medium sized spinning or spincast reel. By getting a reel containing 6 or more bearings, it's more likely to handle a lot of casting and the occasional big fish without issues. That new line can be 6-8 pound test, provided the reel has a properly adjusted drag. The time to adjust it is <u>before</u> you hook into that monster.

Not surprisingly, lures that imitate minnows tend to work well in the Boundary Waters. Trolling a flashy spoon can attract both pike and lake trout. Bring a couple sizes and patterns. As the season progresses and those species move to deeper, cooler water, trolling a deep diving plug such as a ThunderStick will get your offering down where it needs to be.

Shallower diving crankbaits such as a Shad Rap can be trolled or cast near structure in early summer for smallmouth. When bass are "on the nest" (typically early June) surface baits can bring one explosive hit after another.

About half the tackle Blayne takes on his trips is related to a vertical presentation. This might be as simple as hooks and weights for dropping live bait (BWCAW only) near a rocky shoreline. He also brings an array of jig heads to be rigged with plastics such as curly tails. They can be worked at different

25

depths to find "smallies," or kept within a foot of the bottom to entice walleye.

As with fishing anywhere, vary your presentation, lures and location until you find a combination that works. The plus with the Boundary Waters is that you're immersed in a beautiful wilderness setting while you figure out your best approach.

Courtesy Williams and Hall Outfitters

Chapter 4: Safety

No matter how much assistance you get from books and an outfitter, sooner or later you're on your own, in an actual wilderness. While travel through the Boundary Waters is generally safe, there are inherent risks. This is not the time to take unnecessary chances. You probably won't have cell phone coverage and will be hours, if not days, from help.

Only you can decide what risks are appropriate for you. Only you can decide if you have the skills and ability to handle, not only the trip in general, but unique unforeseen circumstances that may arise. Do not consider this, or any guide, a complete list of issues to consider. "That guy never said to get my aluminum boat off the lake during a thunderstorm."

Water Safety: Assuming everyone is comfortable and competent in a canoe, travel is pretty safe. If someone is not, they need to take a class and/or spend some time paddling before the trip. When you get to a portage, use it. Don't run any rapids unless you are absolutely sure you can handle them with ease. When it gets windy, waves get uncomfortably large on the bigger lakes. Don't tempt fate. Wait it out, fish from shore or on the lee side of an island. And although I've been guilty of this one, don't use your PFD (life jacket) as a seat cushion; wear it. You're already a "bad ass" by traveling in the wilderness. There's no need to needlessly risk your life while you're at it.

Packing the canoe is another safety consideration. Some weight, low in the canoe will actually improve stability. Too much weight, especially piled high, does the opposite. All boats should have a Coast Guard approved weight limit visible on the craft. Don't exceed it. Strive to keep the load low in the boat and distributed evenly so the canoe floats on "an even keel."

Advice varies as to whether or not to tie the packs into the boat; usually depending upon conditions. It makes sense to help keep the "cargo" together in the event the canoed is flipped out on a lake. On the other hand, when traveling on moving water, those same ropes could become an entanglement danger.

In the spring and fall when the water is cold, consider staying near shore in less than perfect conditions. Rolling the boat 50 feet from shore in cold water will probably result in an uncomfortable afternoon and an entertaining story you tell for years. Doing the same thing a quarter mile from shore in high waves might become a sad story somebody else tells about you. Common sense and caution will go a long way to make sure the trip is safe and enjoyable.

Speaking of common sense and caution, don't leave your boat unattended when on shore. Unless you are right with the boat, get it out of the water and tie it to something solid. Be extra cautious if you are on an island campsite as watching your only mode of transportation float away can make for a bad day.

Giardia and other waterborne illnesses: Many people traveling through the Boundary Waters drink the water straight out of the lakes with no ill effects whatsoever. My personal feeling, whether I'm canoe camping in Canada or backpacking through the Rocky Mountains, is that the time and effort required to purify my drinking water is a small price to pay to avoid the chance of spending my hard-earned vacation dealing with diarrhea. I can't imagine much joy in a trip to Quetico spent digging hole after hole in a gut-wrenching panic. When I want to gamble, I play in the stock market, not with my health.

There are plenty of options. Filters with a pore size small enough to stop both Giardia and Cryptosporidium are in stock at most outdoor stores. Iodine or chlorine tablets also render water safe to drink as long as they are given the proper amount of time to work. If you like to count on electronics there's even a product called SteriPen that sterilizes the bad critters in your water in moments. And, of course, there's the fallback if all else fails; boil it for a minute. It's foolproof. Bring and use hand sanitizer too. Once again: cheap insurance.

Speaking of water, make sure your extra clothes and other essentials are kept in waterproof bags. Rolling the boat and an unplanned swim is a much bigger deal if your matches are ruined and you don't have any dry clothes to change into.

Bears: A sighting of a bear along the shore or off in the distant woods can be a highlight of the trip. A bear in camp stealing your food is a whole other issue. Bears are rarely a safety issue in the Boundary Waters and you can help keep it that way. Don't leave any food unattended. Don't bring food into your tent. Take all food and anything that smells like food and bear bag it. Basically, keep the food in a bag or pack that is suspended from a tree branch. Keep it at least ten feet in the air and six feet out from the trunk. Do this even if you are on an island campsite. Bears can swim and the mice and chipmunks (more likely culprits) won't have to.

First Aid: If you play outside among rocks and trees, sooner or later somebody will get injured. A first aid kit and some basic knowledge can come in pretty handy when that time arrives. Though they can't handle every situation, a small kit with an assortment of bandages, antiseptic wipes, pain medication and the like should handle most cuts or scrapes encountered. Include Imodium if you insist on ignoring my water purification advice.

Communication: Smart phones are amazing pieces of technology. Many folks count on them all day every day for communication, directions, safety and watching cat videos. Do not count on them here. Cell service is spotty and there are no electrical outlets handy once you've drained the battery on cat videos. Besides, one of the benefits of a wilderness trip is actually getting "unplugged" for a while.

Even if you decide to use a phone or GPS device to navigate through the wilderness, also bring maps, a compass and know how to use them. The batteries won't go bad on a compass and if you drop your map on a rock, it will still work.

Notice the map is handy and in a waterproof bag

That all being said, there are still electronics to consider for both your safety and the peace of mind of those back home. When I go out into the Boundary Waters or on a backpacking trip, especially if I'm going solo, I bring a Spot Satellite Messenger.

This piece of equipment only weighs five ounces, but adds a layer of safety hard to get any other way. The Spot can send prewritten texts or emails from nearly anywhere in the world, including all of the BWCAW and Quetico. I use it as follows. The OK button is used once a day to send a message that everything is fine. It also includes a Google map of my location. There's a second message that I've used to alert folks that I'll be back out of the wilderness the next day. There's a helping hand button I would use if I got hopelessly lost or had a nonlife-threatening injury that kept me from getting out on my own. The message would ask the recipients to contact the outfitter or local police to alert them to my situation and location.

The SOS button is when you need the Calvary. For example, an actual life-threatening injury. Pushing that button sends a distress signal straight to a nearby Search and Rescue. They also get your exact location so there is no search, just rescue, Thankfully, I've never needed either assistance button, but it's nice to know they're there. Just remember, the SOS button is for an actual life-threatening emergency. It is not for use just because you are sick of paddling or really need a pizza.

Garmin now makes a similar product that allows two-way texting. Also, an actual satellite phone can be purchased or rented. Hopefully, you'll never need any of these products, but they are worth considering. If you go to the trouble of purchasing or renting one of these pieces of equipment, be sure to keep it with you. Even a satellite phone is worthless if you are lost or hurt out on a lake and the phone is back at camp. That advice goes for any critical equipment (map, compass, fire starter) that you might need on a day trip away from camp.

Chapter 5: Permits and Regulations

Permits:
If you're working with an outfitter, they can often handle all the details of acquiring a permit. Many are sales agents themselves. Because there are quotas, you want to lock in your reservations as soon as possible for the most popular times (midsummer, holiday weekends). If you're flexible with entry dates and entry points, it's possible to wait until the last minute, but be prepared to be shut out.

For the BWCAW, permits are available on a first come, first serve basis after the annual opening day. (In January, check the website.) You can handle the process yourself through recreation.gov.

Permits for Quetico can be reserved five months in advance. For example, August 1st permits are available on March 1st or later. If you are handling the paperwork yourself, ontarioparks.com is your starting point.

Regulations:
Wilderness travel can free the traveler from many of the rules and regulations that restrict our everyday life. No need to worry about a pesky speed limit when you're out in the canoe. Go as fast as you want! However, it is not all absolutely about personal freedom. To make sure this special place stays special, there are a number of regulations to keep in mind when deciding on, or planning a trip. The following are some highlights of the rules and regulations in force in each area as of this writing.

BWCAW – per Recreation.gov

Travel Permits
- You must enter the BWCAW at the entry point and on the entry date shown on the permit.
- The permit expires when the group leader exits the wilderness.

Group Size
- Nine (9) people and four (4) watercraft are the maximum allowed together in the wilderness.
- You may not exceed the limit at any time or anywhere (on water, portages, campsites) in the BWCAW.

Campfires
- Fires are allowed within the steel fire grates at designated campsites or as specifically approved on your visitor's permit.
- Fire restrictions may be put into effect. Check on current conditions just prior to your trip. You may be required to use a camp stove if there is a campfire restriction.

Campsites
- All members of a permit group must camp together.
- Camp only at Forest Service designated campsites that have steel fire grates and wilderness latrines.
- It is illegal to cut live vegetation for any reason.
- You may camp up to fourteen (14) consecutive days on a specific site.

Miscellaneous
- Leave archaeological, historical, and rock painting sites undisturbed.
- State game laws apply in the BWCAW.
- Dispose of fish remains by traveling well away from campsites, trails, portages and shorelines.
- Fireworks of any kind are illegal.

- Pets must be under control at all times.
- Cans and glass bottles are not allowed. Exceptions are made for non-food containers for items such as fuel, insect repellent and personal toiletries.
- Bathe and wash dishes at least 150 feet from lakes and streams.
- Mechanical assistance through portage wheels is only permitted over the following: International Boundary, Four-Mile Portage, Fall-Newton-Pipestone and Back Bay Portages into Basswood Lake, Prairie Portage, Vermilion-Trout Lake Portage.

Quetico per Ontarioparks.com

Travel Permits
- You must enter Quetico during business hours through the ranger station, on the entry date and entry point designated on your permit. Do not take unnecessary risks, late arrivals due to high winds will be accommodated.

Group Size
- Nine people is the maximum party size allowed on a campsite.

Campfires
- Use existing fire rings. Fire pits must be built on bare rock or bare mineral soil and kept 1.5-3m from vegetation including overhanging trees. Fires are prohibited in a restricted fire zone. Possession or ignition of fireworks in a provincial park is illegal.

Fishing
- Ontario fishing regulations require the use of artificial bait and barbless hooks within Quetico Provincial Park. Live or dead organic bait is not permitted in the park. Examples include leeches, worms and salted minnows.

Barbed hooks may be pinched to conform to regulation. Reduce fish mortality by using barbless hooks, keep fish handling to a minimum, use proper fish handling techniques, and be aware of fishing regulations. A valid Ontario fishing license is required for fishing and must be in your possession. Licenses are not available at all park stations and should be purchased prior to your arrival at www.ontario.ca/fishing

Canoe/Kayaks

- One lifejacket or personal flotation device (PFD) of appropriate size for each person on board
- One buoyant heaving line no less than 15 m (49'3") in length
- One manual propelling device (i.e. set of oars or paddle) or an anchor with no less than 15 m (49'3") of cable, rope or chain in any combination
- One bailer or one manual water pump fitted with or accompanied by sufficient hose
- Sound-signaling device (whistle)
- Watertight flashlight if paddling at night (Batteries must work)

Cultural Sites

- Leave archaeological, historical and pictograph sites untouched. The Pictographs in Quetico are spiritually sacred for Anishinabe People. Approach all pictographs quietly and respectfully. It is illegal to deface these sites or remove objects such as bones, arrowheads, and other artefacts.

Miscellaneous

- It is unlawful to remove, cut or damage any vegetation. For fuel wood, use only fallen dead wood collected from the shoreline and far from your campsite.
- Non-burnable, disposable food and beverage containers are not allowed. Fuel, insect repellent, medicine,

personal toiletry (non-food & beverage) containers are permitted only.

- It is illegal to possess a motorized boat, power saw, gasoline generator or power ice auger in the park. No person may use a mechanized portage device, all terrain vehicle, snowmobile or similar mechanized equipment.
- Pets must be leashed while visiting the park. Non-residents must be able to provide a current vaccination certificate.
- Possession of a firearm, including a rifle, shotgun, handgun, air gun, pellet gun, paintball gun, slingshot, bow or crossbow is prohibited. Hunting, molesting and harassing wildlife is also prohibited.

In addition, it is always a good idea to follow the Principals of Leave No Trace.

Leave No Trace Seven Principles

1. Plan Ahead and Prepare
2. Travel and Camp on Durable Surfaces
3. Dispose of Waste Properly
4. Leave What You Find
5. Minimize Campfire Impacts
6. Respect Wildlife
7. Be Considerate of Other Visitors

(© 1999 by the Leave No Trace Center for Outdoor Ethics: www.LNT.org.)

Chapter 6: Gear

While canoe camping is similar to backpacking, there are important differences in equipment and more flexibility as far as how much weight to bring. Below is a basic equipment list to start the planning process. As mentioned, most outfitters can provide complete outfitting that covers all your camping and traveling needs, or partial outfitting for specific pieces of gear.

A typical complete outfitting package includes:
- Canoe (Plus registration for your own boat if required in your home state)
- Paddles (an extra is a good idea)
- PFDs (Life jackets that fit)
- Tent
- Sleeping bags
- Sleeping pads
- Dining fly
- Packs (designed for use in canoes and on portages)
- Plastic liner bags to waterproof essential equipment
- Ropes to hang food bag plus other various tasks
- Cook kit w plates and eating utensils
- Food
- Stove (quicker and easier than cooking over a fire. In dry weather, there may be a fire ban.)
- Saw and/or small axe if campfires are planned
- Maps for the planned route
- Required permits

Trips into Quetico also include:
- Fire grate
- Trowel (to dig a cat hole)

Personal essentials
- Two sets of clothes (quick dry fabrics can be a plus)
- Fleece or light jacket (hat, gloves, heavier clothes depending on season)
- Shoes/boots that can handle rough trails while carrying a heavy load.
- Rain gear
- Toiletries and medications required
- First aid kit
- Outdoor essentials: extra lighters, knife, compass
- Insect repellant (depending on season)
- Identification: Passport if crossing the border (Quetico)

Optional items
- Camera
- Book and/or journal
- Fishing gear
- Comfort items such as pillows or folding chairs
- Second set of shoes for camp
- Communications such as a Spot Satellite Tracker or Satellite phone.
- Whatever else you are willing to carry in and back out

Weightless items to bring along
- Skill to safely paddle a canoe
- Common sense to know when conditions (wind, storms) warrant "waiting it out"
- Knowledge on how to use a map and compass
- Positive attitude to deal with less than optimal conditions

Chapter 7: How it Really Is

One way I've found that I get a feel for a possible trip is to read about the experience of others on that same journey. Toward that purpose, I've included two previously published articles written about Boundary Waters trips:

This article first appeared in the Boundary Waters Journal

Man Chain Reunion

My brother Bob and I took our first trip to the Boundary Waters together in 1991. Accompanying us on that trip was Bob's 12-year-old son Andy. It was a great trip and Bob and I started a tradition of returning to this special place every other year. As teens are wont to do however, Andy drifted apart from his Dad's interests and showed little desire to return. He had "been there, done that," so we were pleasantly surprised when he asked about joining us for a trip back to canoe country. Enthused by his interest, we worked on short notice and pulled a trip together for September 2001.

After the 15-hour drive from Ohio, we made use of a room and breakfast at Moose Lake's Canadian Border Outfitters – along with a tow to Prairie Portage for our entrance into Quetico. The day was seasonably cool in the morning but clear, with the promise of a warm afternoon. I took it as a good omen when we spotted a bald eagle on Birch Lake, not 20 minutes into the day's paddle.

The beauty we remembered of Emerald Lake from past trips had called us back and we headed directly through Birch and Carp Lakes. The area had received considerable rain of late and the portages were swampy. Emerald was on the edge of the damage from the massive 1999 storm, and the difference between the east and west banks was dramatic. New vegetation had started growing on the eastern shore, but it will be several years before the views of destruction are completely hidden. We set up camp on a small island. The evening was spent cooking steaks and catching and releasing smallmouths while watching one of the most vibrant sunsets I've ever witnessed.

The next morning Bob spotted a family of otters heading across the lake toward our camp. We sat rock still and the otters came within 10 feet of us without ever detecting our presence. Unfortunately, other creatures did notice us: mosquitos. I had camped in this area at this time of year in the past without any problem, but this trip was different. Looking around, we figured out why. Many of the blown down trees had left small craters as their root balls were pulled up. The recent rains had filled the craters, creating pools chock full of mosquito larva, which were eager to join the clouds of their adult cousins at the blood buffet of Andy, Bob and me. Even 100% Deet had little effect. We quickly decided to break camp and head away from the blowdown area into the Man Chain.

The portage out of Emerald wasn't long, but it started straight up for about ten rods and then turned, both literally and figuratively, downhill. The recent rains had turned the trail into a quagmire and the perfect habitat to breed more mosquitoes. A short paddle across an unnamed lake led us to a short, though no more pleasant, portage into That Man Lake.

The end of the portage was like flipping a switch. The day was sunny and warm, with enough breeze on the larger lake to keep the insects at bay. We quickly found a gorgeous campsite on a mid-lake island. The site had a great view, well-suited fishing rock and a refreshing lack of mosquitos. Camp was set up in time for an early afternoon swim and nap. By the time I awoke, the welts on my skin were fast becoming a dim memory (or an experience that builds character). Though it stormed during the night, the weather was perfect and we stayed put — seeing only one other canoe during our stay.

The second morning was foggy and after searching for the source of a clattering noise in the distance, we spotted the ghost of a moose as it meandered along the far shore. Each evening we were treated to a full moon which provided enough light to fish by. The fishing was slow, although we caught enough smallmouth and walleye to keep it interesting.

The fourth day of our trip dawned warm with a strong wind from the southwest, reminding us that we were due back on the following day and needed to cover some distance. We fought the strengthening headwind to the 136-rod portage into Sheridan Lake. I spent the portage formulating plans to replace my heavy aluminum canoe with a Kevlar model. A short paddle and portage later, we were back on Carp heading toward the western end of the lake. Camp was set up on a peninsula within site of the campsite we had used on Andy and Bob's first trip, some ten years earlier. As I took a short swim, the sky turned ugly and the beginning of a cold front hit. For the first time on the trip, we pulled out the tarp and ate under it as several waves of showers passed through.

Just before dark the rains eased off and we fished from the bank. Andy, who had earlier caught the largest walleye of the trip, proceeded to catch the largest smallmouth; both on a spin-jig with a curlytail I had given him. Rigging up a matching lure myself, I soon hooked "the one that got away," a huge northern pike that broke the line on a head-shaking jump.

The temperature was dropping fast so we gave up on the fishing to enjoy a fire on our last evening. As we sat near the flames, we discussed and relived the trip; almost as if it were already completed. Remarkably, the clouds parted just in time for the moonrise to provide a beautiful silver light across the scene – bringing us back to the present with another postcard-perfect memory.

The morning brought fair skies and a warm breeze; great conditions for the return paddle through Birch, Sucker, Newfound and Moose lakes. We arrived back at Canadian Border Outfitters in time for a late lunch of buffalo burgers. At times, conditions on this trip were more difficult than past trips. The advancing ages of the senior members of the party did little to help, but as always, the experience of the North Woods was magical. My memories of Andy as a boy in Quetico were joined by new ones of him as a man, carrying his weight through paddle and portage. He and his dad were closer than I had seen them in years. Best of all, before we had even driven back to Ohio, Andy talked of returning with us to the Boundary Waters.

Chapter 8: Solo Adventure

This article first appeared in Canoeing.com

Old versus New

What greeted me as I delved into the packaging was, "Welcome. Opening this box is the first step to making sure you don't come home in one." Maybe there were good reasons to join the 21st century after all.

I have always thought of myself as an old-fashioned kind of guy. I paddle a wooden canoe, don't know how Facebook works; I even have a working 8-track tape player (though finding new tapes is getting tough). Unfortunately, having recently turned 50, I was feeling not so much old-fashioned, but just old. In looking for a way to reaffirm my abilities and self-reliance, I began to mentally search for a personal challenge. Having visited the Boundary Waters many times over the previous twenty years, I knew the challenges and rewards of a trip to the Boreal Forest.

To transform a trip there into more of a personal challenge, I considered, for the first time, a solo trip. I could spend some time being totally self-reliant including outfitting myself, using my wooden solo canoe that I had built twenty years before. By going after Labor Day, I was sure there would be plenty of solitude.

While up for a challenge, I wasn't looking to put my life on the line unnecessarily. Since the trip would be in September, not seeing other parties for days at a time was likely. My biggest worry was to be sick or injured with no one to help or get help. Despite being proudly old-fashioned, I found myself opening a box containing a Spot Satellite Personal Tracker.

The Spot weighs half a pound (now even less) and can send prewritten text messages or emails, along with a Google map of the sender's location, from nearly anywhere to preselected phone numbers and email addresses. You can send an "OK" message or an "I need help" message. In an emergency situation, a 911 message can be sent directly to the closest Search and Rescue. The cost of the unit, along with a year's worth of service, was approximately $250. Michelle, my wife, while supportive of the trip, was plainly worried. While I knew the chances of needing the unit were remote, I did not want my last thoughts to be, "Why didn't you spend the money you cheap dumb ass?"

Set up was simple, even for a technologically challenged person. The OK message was simply, "I'm OK. Here's a map of where I am." The Help message was a bit more detailed. "Things aren't going quite as planned. While I'm not in danger, I need help to get out. Please call xxx with my location." The 911 message is set; you just provide contact phone numbers to be sent along to the nearest Search and Rescue. I had the OK and Help messages set to be sent to Michelle and my brother Bob, who had joined me on Boundary Waters trips in the past. Bob, the typically optimistic member of the family, ask that I keep the Spot on me as I double portaged. "The last thing you want is to get a compound leg fracture and have that Spot thing a quarter mile away with the other load." While a compound fracture was pretty low on the list of what I want regardless of the situation, it was a point well taken. The Spot would remain with me at all times.

The non-technical portion of the preparation went smoothly and I arrived at Williams & Hall Outfitters near Ely, Minnesota the afternoon before Labor Day. The route was to be pretty open, a motor tow to the Birch Lake portage, travel to Knife Lake and then several options for a few days were laid out depending on weather and my speed of travel. My boat is stable, maybe a little slow, though I'd never carried much weight in it before.

After a fairly sleepless night, dawn breaks on a beautiful morning that promises a following breeze to assist with my travels. As we travel up Moose Lake towards Birch, Blayne Hall, the outfitter's owner, veers the motorboat to show me some roosting eagles. Surrounded by the beauty of the day, my trepidation of a solo trip vanishes. After trading farewells, I begin my journey hoping to find a challenge, solitude and a few fish in a beautiful wilderness.

Paddling east on Birch Lake I immediately notice, even with a bit of a tailwind, how slow the loaded boat is. The beautiful weather more than makes up for the pace and, double portaging, I'm through Birch to Carp and then the smaller lakes of Melon and Seed by lunch. Though my stamina is being sapped by the slow, hard paddling, I continue on through Portage Lake and into Knife by early afternoon. I pull into South Bay and pick a gorgeous campsite tucked well back in a small cove out of the way. I had seen a few other parties during the day, but they all appeared to be heading in, ending their trips on the holiday. After setting up camp, I cool off with a swim, send out an OK message with the Spot and leisurely prepare a steak dinner to cap off the day.

After a good night's sleep, I awake to broken clouds and a steady wind from the southwest. Gathering together lunch, camera, rain gear and fishing gear, I set out for Dix Lake to cast for pike. Even with a short stop to take a few shots of an eagle perched on a tall pine, I cover the 4 miles to the high overlook near the Bonnie Lake portage in well under an hour. The view west is tremendous even though the clouds are becoming solid and hanging lower. With the wind picking up I'm glad to portage into Bonnie and get off the big water of Knife. Two more relatively short portages have me on Dix Lake where I eat lunch, send an OK message with the Spot and cast for uncooperative pike.

The rain, which had threatened for a while is now coming down in waves. I have two options for getting back to camp. I can take three short portages back to Knife and fight the wind on big water, or take five portages that total over 500 rods and return through Vera Lake. Not a fan of long, steep portages in the rain, I convince myself the wind is easing off and head back through Bonnie.

Once back on Knife, the wind, of course, picks up in intensity. I cinch the life jacket up tight, and paddling for all I'm worth, fight from island to island. At each open water crossing, I yell encouragement to myself to keep up the adrenaline level. The boat is stable through the waves, but progress is painfully slow. The closer I get to camp, the more the wind and waves conspire to slow my progress. After three hours on Knife, soaked and tired to the bone, I finally make it back to camp. Challenge is checked off the to-do list. After dinner under the tarp and a visit to the flask to settle nerves, it's an early night.

The rain comes down on and off all night, ending for good around dawn. I decide not to move camp, but instead spend the day drying out and exploring the area. As often happens after a strong storm, the sky clears, turning the day picture perfect. I leisurely check out Portage Lake and also Vera Lake, sending an OK message from there while lying on the bank in the warm sun. Back at the campsite by mid-afternoon I'm joined in the cove by a family of loons. They're followed by a group of five river otters that spend over an hour oblivious to my presence, frolicking, fishing and generally putting on a show. Sitting and watching their antics, I realize I haven't seen another person since the first day. Solitude is mentally checked off the list.

Catching a few fish remain on my to-do list and so I paddle to a nearby steep, rocky shoreline to cast a jig for smallmouth. My first cast results in a chunky, foot long fighter. As the second cast hits the now calm water, an eagle that had been perched unnoticed nearby is spooked. It glides down near the canoe before flying off to a new perch overlooking camp. The beautiful sunset is spent catching and releasing eager smallies. None are bragging size, but they fill the bill perfectly.

I awake early on day four refreshed and ready to travel. Since I'm paddling back to the outfitters without the benefit of a tow, the plan is to move closer to Moose Lake, paddling until the inevitable head winds start. I'd like to make it a shorter trip out the next day. Not relishing a re-enactment of the battle against the wind with a boatload of equipment, I push off shortly after dawn with the air dead-still and Knife Lake mirror smooth.

Portaging through Seed and Melon Lakes, the air stays calm and the only ripples on the water are made by each lake's resident beaver as they pass near the canoe on their morning rounds. By midmorning I'm on Carp Lake. Since Bob and I had camped there years before with his sons, I sent an OK message as I travel through.

What I didn't know until my return was that Bob & Michelle are trading emails with each Spot message I send, discussing my progress and dispelling Michelle's concerns. "Jim looks like he's in the middle of the lake. Do you think he's in his boat?" "If he's not, I doubt he would be sending the OK. I know exactly where he is. We were there…"

It's not until Birch Lake that there is the first hint of a breeze, and it's a tailwind! Can I be that lucky? It appears that every site on Birch is empty, but with a tailwind, the urge to keep moving takes over. Lunch is spent on a high bank overlooking Sucker Lake and several eagle roosts. I'm only a couple hours from the take out. The sky is partly cloudy, the temperature about 60 degrees with a light wind out of the northeast; perfect conditions for travel with a slow boat. Pushing on, I cross Sucker, Newfound and Moose Lake to arrive at Williams & Hall in mid-afternoon. After a cold refreshment and a recap of the trip, it's time to load up and start the long drive home. While the trip isn't exactly what was anticipated, it is exactly what I need.

The Spot Messenger, while not fitting in with my "old-fashioned" self-image, was a worthwhile tool to ease both my mind and Michelle's. There is no doubt that on a solo trip, or any trip with one canoe, the Spot could be a lifesaver. Maybe I'm not as old-fashioned as I think. Next time, perhaps a Kevlar boat? Hmm, something to think about.

Chapter 9: Next Steps

Hopefully this short introduction to the Boundary Waters has whet your appetite to visit, or at least gather more data. There are many sources of information to continue the planning process. If you have specific questions about the material in this book, feel free to email me at jim@oldmanoutdoors.net.

Outfitters in the Boundary Waters area have been extremely helpful to me on past trips. I've worked with three personally and all were positive experiences. Those are:

- Williams and Hall Outfitters at www.williamsandhall.com
- Canadian Border Outfitters at www.canoetrip.com
- Zups Canoe Outfitter at www.zupsresort.com

For a magazine that is filled from cover to cover with Boundary Waters adventures and information, try The Boundary Waters Journal. Their website is www.boundarywatersjournal.com.

Numerous books have been written about various aspects of the BWCAW and Quetico. History, travel guides and fishing guides can all be had to provide more in-depth information about this special place. The Boundary Waters Journal carries several titles and, of course, there's always Amazon.

For thousands of years, humans lived comfortably in the wilderness. These experiences made us who we are and shaped our very DNA. By contrast, today's fast paced lives are full of stressful, yet forgettable events. Consider making your next real experience memorable. Feed your DNA. Visit the Boundary Waters. Visit the wilderness.

Wilderness is more than lakes, rivers, and timber along the shores, more than fishing or just camping. It is the sense of the primeval, of space, solitude, silence and the eternal mystery. (Sigurd Olson)

58173818R00033

Made in the USA
Middletown, DE
05 August 2019